WRITING AND STAGING

Funny Plays

Charlotte Guillain

capstone

© 2016 Heinemann-Raintree
an imprint of Capstone Global Library, LLC
Chicago, Illinois

To contact Capstone Global Library please call 800-747-4992, or visit our web site
www.capstonepub.com

Edited by James Benefield
Designed by Philippa Jenkins
Original illustrations © Capstone Global Library Limited 2016
Picture research by Kelly Garvin
Production by Victoria Fitzgerald
Originated by Capstone Global Library Ltd
Printed and bound in China

19 18 17 16 15
10 9 8 7 6 5 4 3 2 1

Library of Congress Cataloging-in-Publication Data
Cataloging-in-publication data is available at the Library of Congress.
ISBN 978 1 4846 2769 3 (hardback)
ISBN 978 1 4846 2773 0 (paperback)
ISBN 978 1 4846 2777 8 (ebook PDF)

Acknowledgments
Photo credits: Alamy: Hill Street Studios/Blend Images, 22, Kumar Sriskandan, 40; Capstone Press/Karon Dubke, cover, 24, 25, 38; Corbis: Hill Street Studios/Blend Images, 6, 20, 26, Peter M. Fisher, 28, Robbie Jack, 14, 18, 32, 39, Tomas Rodriguez, 43; Getty Images: Dirk Anschutz, 9, Jupiter Images, 30, Kevin Cummins, 34; Glow Images: Heiner Heine, 37, Rubberball/Alan Bailey, 15, Ulrich Doering, 21; iStockphoto: digitalskillet, 10, Juanmonino, 42, ozgurdonmaz, 4, PeopleImages, 8; Shutterstock: ArtFamily, 33, bluedogroom, 31, Christian Bertrand, 27, digitalreflections, 35, karen roach, 16, Matt Ragen, 29, nvelichko, 13, PAISAN HOMHUAN, 12, Paolo Bona, 5, wavebreakmedia, 36.

Artistic elements: Shutterstock/3DDock.

We would like to thank Mike Gould for his invaluable help with the preparation of this book.

Every effort has been made to contact copyright holders of any material reproduced in this book. Any omissions will be rectified in subsequent printings if notice is given to the publisher.

CONTENTS

Some words are shown in bold, **like this**. You can find out what they mean by looking in the glossary.

WHAT IS A PLAY?

People all over the world have been telling each other stories for thousands of years. Stories can make us cry, think, or laugh.

We have many different ways of sharing stories. For example, a storyteller can charm an audience with a story he or she tells from memory. Many of us enjoy reading stories in novels and comics, and lots of the shows we watch on television tell us a story. Some of the most popular stories make us laugh.

A play is a story

A play is another way to tell a story. A play usually starts life as a **script**. A group of actors work together to perform a version of the script in front of a live audience. Meanwhile, many people work hard behind the scenes to make the play run smoothly. These people often include a **director**, a **set** designer, sound and lighting engineers, and people in charge of costumes and **props**.

People love to watch funny characters in a play.

Some people write plays for a living. Others become professional actors or directors or get a job working backstage in a theater. Many people enjoy performing in plays for fun, and many schools give their students the chance to be involved in drama. Plays can be performed in many different places, from world-famous theaters in big cities to school auditoriums and community centers. Some plays are even performed outdoors!

Some of the most famous plays are funny. They are called **comedies**. William Shakespeare wrote many well-known comedies, including *A Midsummer Night's Dream* and *Twelfth Night.* His comedies often involve mistaken identity and characters disguising themselves as the opposite sex. Shakespeare also played around with language in funny ways in his comedies. His characters often find themselves in complicated situations, and the audience finds it amusing to watch them untangle themselves from these **plots**.

Both actors and the audience love a play in the open air— as long as it's not raining!

WHAT IS A SCRIPT?

The person who creates a script is called a **playwright**. One of the main ways he or she tells a story is through words, or **dialogue**, spoken by the actors.

Play scripts are written in a different way than other types of writing. The text is written with the characters' names appearing on the left-hand side, to indicate whose turn it is to speak. A colon appears after the name, followed by the words that the character has to say. For example:

character   dialogue

AMY: That dog has no nose!

JAMAL: How does he smell?

AMY: Pretty awful, actually!

Writing Tip

Just as a novel is divided up into chapters, a play is usually divided up into sections called acts. A full-length play is made up of least two acts, with a number of scenes within each act. Plays with just one act will have several different scenes.

Actors read the script to see what they are going to do and say in the play.

In addition to the character names and their dialogue, the playwright also includes **stage directions** in the script. These tell the actors when and how to speak and move. These directions are usually in parenthesis and italics *(like this)*, so they stand out clearly from the dialogue. For example:

JAMAL: I'd love to take that dog home...

AMY: But you own two already!

JAMAL: Hmmm... *(looks up, thinking)* — stage direction
(The dog is sitting, looking cute)
(sighs) Maybe I can dress him up as a cat. Do you think the other dogs would notice?

TRY IT

Some actors don't use a script at all! They make up their own **sketch**, following a basic story. This is called **improvisation**.

7

COMEDIES

Playwrights use a range of comedy and characters to get their audience laughing.

Visual comedy

Visual comedy works very well on the stage. **Slapstick** is a type of visual comedy where the actors behave in overdramatic ways when doing something, like slipping on a banana peel or running into something such as a wall. It's funny because the actors are exaggerating their movements and reactions, and nobody gets seriously hurt.

Matilda the Musical is based on the book by Roald Dahl. It is full of funny songs and amazing visual comedy because the characters perform **acrobatics**, Miss Trunchbull rampages across the stage, and Matilda plays tricks on some of the horrible grown-up characters.

When actors perform slapstick well, it can usually make the audience laugh.

It is good to have a mix of different types of comedy to amuse as much of your audience as possible.

Mistaken identity

Mistaken identity is another feature of many comedies. For example, in *The Importance of Being Earnest* by Oscar Wilde, the lead character is a respectable man named Jack Worthing. Jack pretends to have a brother named Ernest, who is always getting into scrapes. In fact, Ernest and Jack are the same person! People in the city know him as Ernest, but friends in the country know him as Jack. When these two worlds meet, the result is very funny.

Wordplay

Playwrights also use **wordplay** in comedies. Many words or phrases can have more than one meaning, or words can sound the same but have a different spelling and meaning. Many playwrights write jokes, called puns, based on wordplay, to make their audience laugh. Characters often say the wrong words in a sentence, which can be funny, especially if the character thinks he or she is very important.

Other features of a comedy include running jokes that the audience starts to expect and **catchphrases** that certain characters use again and again. Actors also use **comic timing** to react or go on- and offstage at just the right moment to make the audience laugh.

Ideas for comedy

If you decide to write and stage a comic play, think about what you could base it on. Perhaps there was a funny situation from your own life when something went wrong. Maybe you could think about some funny books you have read and base your script on one of those. Many comedies mix humor with other emotions to give the audience a more complex experience, but they nearly always have a happy ending.

Before you choose your story, think about how many actors you'll need or how many friends want to be involved. You'll want to have enough **parts** and jobs for everyone, but you don't want to be overwhelmed by too many characters!

Alice's Adventures in Wonderland is a great story for a comedy. It is mostly nonsense, and a lot of the humor comes from fantastical situations, wordplay, and slapstick. If you're basing your play on a book or part of a story, it might help to start by mapping the story.

Take some time to think and read to get inspiration for your play.

Alice's Adventures in Wonderland story map

Alice follows a white rabbit down a rabbit hole. She shrinks and then grows.

Giant Alice cries and makes a flood. She shrinks again and swims after a mouse.

Alice meets other animals and they have a **Caucus Race** to get dry.

The white rabbit sends Alice into a house, but she grows again. She eats cakes to shrink again.

Alice meets the Duchess, whose baby turns into a pig! She also meets the Cheshire Cat.

Alice meets a caterpillar and eats pieces of a mushroom to get back to her normal size.

Alice meets the Queen of Hearts, who wants to chop everyone's heads off!

Alice arrives at a mad tea party and meets the Hatter, the March Hare, and a Dormouse.

Alice meets a Gryphon and then a Mock Turtle, who tells her his story. Then they dance.

At a trial, the Knave of Hearts is accused of stealing the Queen's tarts. Alice argues with the Queen and then wakes up.

Creating funny characters

Each character in a funny play needs to be different and have a clear personality. Funny plays can have certain types of characters, such as these:

The main or "straight" character

"Straight" and ordinary, he or she doesn't make many jokes or take part in slapstick. Many funny moments come from this character's reaction to other characters in the play.

The joker

This character finds everything funny. Often he or she is the main character's **sidekick**. The joker might use certain expressions or catchphrases a lot.

The "bad guy" or bully

Funny plays often also include a villain, bully, or someone who thinks he or she is better than everyone else. It's funny when this character is made to look silly.

The "fall guy"

This character often gets blamed for everything that goes wrong. He or she frequently doesn't understand what's going on around him or her.

You can see some of these typical characters in the *Shrek* movies. Shrek is the straight man in the main **role**. Donkey is his joker sidekick, and Lord Farquaad and Prince Charming are bad guys.

Characters in *Alice's Adventures in Wonderland*

It's helpful to list the characters in your play and make notes about them. Here are the characters in the Mad Tea-Party scene in *Alice*:

Alice
A straight character, she can't understand the chaos going on around her and wants to make sense of everything. Her misunderstandings and mistakes are part of the comedy.

The March Hare
He supports the Hatter, helping to set up situations for him to tell jokes.

The Hatter
The joker, who tells lots of crazy stories, has the **punchlines** to all the jokes, and is rude to Alice. This is funny because we don't normally expect people to speak to each other like that.

The Dormouse
This is the fall guy who is picked on by the Hatter and March Hare. He gets shoved in the teapot at the end!

The Hatter is the joker of the story.

13

TELLING THE STORY

Once you have your story map and characters figured out, you can start working on the details of your play. When you begin writing a comedy, there are some things you need to consider.

Explaining the plot

It can be useful to include a central character to explain parts of the story that aren't acted out onstage. This is useful if your story involves magic or travel. This can be done by a separate **narrator** or just another character from the play.

This person can also make comments about what is going on. In a comedy, he or she can be funny by interrupting or pausing the flow of the action for comic effect. This reminds people in the audience that what they are watching is only a story. It also helps to keep things lighthearted. If you are using a separate narrator who is not a character, he or she could sit or stand at the side of the stage. This way, the narrator is kept out of the way of the action.

Many traditional comedies—from Shakespeare's time to today—have a happy ending. Sometimes the characters fall in love or get married at the end of the play. In any case, the plays normally end with a big celebration.

Characters fall in love in many traditional comedies.

Using a narrator in *Alice's Adventures in Wonderland*

Because much of the story in *Alice's Adventures in Wonderland* is nonsense, the audience can often get very confused about what is happening! A narrator would therefore help the audience follow the story. For example, as you go into the scene with the Mad Tea-Party, the narrator could link it from the previous scene:

You can change the pace of the play when a character talks to the audience directly.

NARRATOR: Alice was a bit shocked when that baby turned into a pig! She's also getting tired and hungry, so she's glad when she finds that the Cheshire Cat has sent her to a tea party. The table is set, but this is no ordinary tea party…

ALICE: That dormouse doesn't look very comfortable with the others resting their elbows on it. I wonder if I could sit down for some tea.

MARCH HARE
AND HATTER: *(in unison)* No room! No room!

The structure of your script

Most stories have a beginning, middle, and end. A script also needs this shape, or structure. If your play is less than 15 or 20 minutes long, you'll only need one act. If it's longer, you might want more than one act, with each act divided up into different scenes.

For example, in the first act, you could introduce the main characters and explain to the audience what your main character wants. In the second act, your hero will often face a difficult challenge or problem. In the third act, the hero might solve this problem and find happiness by the end of the play.

Take some time to plan your play before you start to write it.

Ideas for structuring *Alice's Adventures in Wonderland* play

At the start of the first act, introduce Alice to the audience: show what sort of person she is.

Include several scenes to show Alice shrinking and growing, to help the audience understand her feeling confused and out of place.

Or end the first half of the play with the Cheshire Cat sending Alice to the March Hare's house.

Consider having an **intermission** after Alice visits the Duchess's house, where her baby turns into a pig.

Use the intermission to set up the stage for the tea party, so that the second half of the play—the new act—could begin with the Mad Tea-Party.

Use the second half of the play to build up the atmosphere for the trial scene, when Alice finally stands up for herself.

The play ends happily when Alice wakes up back in the real world.

Lots of the dialogue in *Matilda the Musical* sounds like the words Roald Dahl used in his original story.

Dealing with dialogue

Apart from stage directions, all the language in a play is dialogue. If your play is based on a book, make sure the dialogue stays similar to what the characters would say in the book. If you are making up a story, make sure each character's words sound like natural speech. You can check this by reading the **lines** aloud to a friend.

These catchphrases from books and movies are memorable:
- In the *Harry Potter* series, the character Hagrid often says, "I probably shouldn't have told you that" when he's said too much!
- Buzz Lightyear from the *Toy Story* movies has the catchphrase "To infinity and beyond!"

Some characters in your play may have special ways of talking. For example, a comic character might speak quickly or slowly. Some characters might only speak in short sentences, while others might babble on endlessly. Giving each of your characters a different way of speaking helps to make them distinct from one another. You could also give certain characters funny catchphrases. These will make the characters more memorable for the audience.

Dialogue in *Alice's Adventures*

The dialogue in *Alice's Adventures in Wonderland* is distinctive. Because the book was written in the 19th century, some of the language may seem old-fashioned to us. Also, some of the characters seem to speak in complete nonsense! However, if your play is based on a book, it's a good idea to follow the text of the original story when you write your dialogue. This is because your audience may be expecting a certain style.

Below is an example of how the dialogue in your version of *Alice* might look:

ALICE:	That dormouse doesn't look very comfortable with the others resting their elbows on it. I wonder if I could sit down for some tea.
MARCH HARE AND HATTER:	*(in unison)* No room! No room!
ALICE:	*(indignantly)* There's plenty of room!
	(She sits in a large armchair)
MARCH HARE:	Have some cake.
ALICE:	I don't see any cake.
MARCH HARE:	There isn't any.
ALICE:	*(angrily)* Then it wasn't very civil of you to offer it.

TAKING THE LEAD

Once the script has been written, the next step is to get a team together to stage the play.

The director's role

A director takes the lead in staging the play. First, he or she chooses who will play each character. Then, when rehearsals begin, the director watches from the front. He or she helps the actors to stand in the best place on the stage, speak, and move around well.

As the director, you will work with all members of the team. For example, you will work with the play's designer to decide what the set will look like. You will work with other members of the team to decide what costumes and props are needed.

It's important for the actors to listen to the director. He or she has a vision for how the play will work.

The director might get the actors to try acting a scene several ways before making a decision.

Tips on starting out as the director of *Alice's Adventures*

1. First, get to know the original book and the characters well. You should make a note of any problems you may have about the story for discussions later.

2. Next, read the script several times. Think about the actors you know who may be good for each part. What ideas do you have about sets and costumes? How will you create the special effects to show Alice shrinking and growing?

3. Talk to the set designer and costume manager and figure out how the scenes will look and how you will dress the characters. Try to keep things simple and use very few props, or it could get complicated and expensive.

4. Encourage anyone who wants to act in the play to read the script and perhaps the original story, too, to help them tell the story the right way onstage.

5. You're now ready to **cast** your play!

THEATER JOB

A good director needs to be a good leader. It's important that everyone listens to the director so that the team works together. However, he or she also needs to be sensitive to other people's feelings and support actors who may be struggling. A good director knows what everyone's job involves and is always ready to solve any problems that come up.

Actors can audition for more than one part if they want to.

Casting a play

The director usually casts the play. This means finding and choosing actors for the characters, or parts. It's important to choose someone who is right for the part. The actor should feel comfortable performing his or her character and be able to bring the dialogue to life. Actors usually **audition** for a part they really want. They read or perform a small section from the play in front of the director. After everyone has auditioned, the director can decide who will play each part.

TRY IT

Do characters in your comedy need to do physical slapstick or acrobatics? If so, you will need actors who are skilled in dance or gymnastics for these roles.

In a comedy, some characters may have certain physical features that the director needs to consider. For example, if a character is particularly tall or short, the actor will need to be the right size. Of course, makeup, costumes, wigs, and masks can help actors look like the characters they are playing.

Casting *Alice's Adventures*

Think about the following when casting a play based on *Alice's Adventures in Wonderland*:

Alice
* She's the main character, so choose a reliable person. She needs to attend all rehearsals and learn lots of lines.

* She needs to be a confident actor who can get along with everyone on the team.

The Hatter
* This character should be an actor who likes being silly!

* He needs to work well with the actors playing the March Hare and the Dormouse. These three share many scenes together.

* Good comic timing is also important.

The Queen of Hearts
* This character shouts a lot and can be scary. Choose an actor with a strong voice and who enjoys terrifying other people!

The Gryphon and the Mock Turtle
* These characters have to dance onstage. Choose actors who enjoy dancing.

23

ACTING IN A COMEDY

When the play has been cast, the actors should get to know the parts they are going to play. One way is to start practicing as a team.

Improvisation

Actors should think about how their characters speak and move before they start rehearsing the play. One way to do this is to try some improvisation games at the start of rehearsals.

Improvisation is when actors perform without reading from a script. Instead, they think about the character they are playing and make up little scenes with each other while still pretending to be that character. Sometimes improvisation is actually built into the play. For example, the method of going "off-script" is often used in comedies.

"Stop and Talk"

As a director, it is your job to help your actors to get to know their characters. You can do this by playing the following improvisation game with them. You need a bell for this game.

It is useful to talk through your characters with one another. However, you could also improvise.

Try improvising a scene set in a street.

Before you start:

1. Tell the actors to think carefully about how their characters would move in different situations. This could be when walking down the street, running to catch a bus, or moving around at a party.

2. Now ask them to think about how their characters would speak in these situations. What words or tone of voice would they use?

To play the game:

1. Think of a situation (for example, a busy store) and tell everyone what it is.

2. Ring your bell. At the sound of this, everyone starts moving around the room.

3. After 10 seconds, ring your bell again. Everyone should stop and stand still.

4. At this point, you need to suggest a question. Your actors must then talk to the person closest to them about it. It could be anything from "What are you most happy with or scared of?" to "Who do you like or hate the most?" Each actor must give an answer quickly, in character.

5. When you see that everyone has answered the question, ring your bell again. Repeat the game with a new situation.

Rehearsing

As the director, you need your team to practice performing the play. Everyone needs to become familiar with what he or she is doing. This means rehearsing! Agree in advance to the days and times when everyone can get together. You need to be good at communicating with your whole team. It is important to motivate everyone to stay committed to all the rehearsals.

TRY IT

Set up a timetable so that everyone knows when rehearsals are taking place far in advance. If you don't need everyone for a particular rehearsal, highlight the names of those who should be there. It is important for people to easily see when they are needed. Remember to include some breaks in between rehearsals, too.

You might break into smaller groups to rehearse certain scenes.

You might spend a lot of time deciding how you all move together on the stage.

Start your rehearsals by sitting and reading the script together in the same room. After this, you can move to a bigger space where everyone can move around. Remember, you may not always be able to rehearse in the same place you will use for performances.

Sometimes you may want to run through the whole play. Other times, it may be better to focus on key scenes. It can often be boring for the actors to keep repeating the same lines or sit and wait for their time to rehearse. However, showing up for rehearsals is the only way to make the performance smooth and enjoyable for an audience.

Comic timing

In a comedy, timing is very important. If a character is about to tell a joke, but the audience hasn't finished laughing about something else, the actor should wait. The audience needs to be quiet so any other joke can be heard. If the actor does not wait, a comic moment will be missed.

If a scene requires one actor to come onstage the same moment that another leaves, the actors must time this properly. It takes practice, and the actors must get used to listening to **cues**. A joke can fall flat if the actors react too early or late.

BEHIND THE SCENES

As the director, you need to think about what goes on behind the scenes of your play. This means figuring out things like a set, costumes, props, lighting, and sound.

Ideas for designing a set

Your play will need a set to show where the action takes place. This is sometimes called the scenery. It doesn't have to be complicated to be effective!

You could hang up curtains or large pieces of painted cardboard to show the play's setting. Whatever you do, make sure the set is not too heavy to move around. You will need to set up items and take them down quickly over the course of the performance, as the location of the action may change.

TRY IT

Some professional theaters use special features, such as trapdoors, when performing comedies. Characters can pop out of the floor suddenly and surprise the audience! Have you considered having characters in your play do something similar for comic effect?

Another reason to keep your set simple is because you don't want your audience to be distracted by it. Consider painting the entire background green to show a forest, or just paint the area where the action is taking place.

In a professional theater, a set designer creates a design for the scenery and supervises its construction.

A simple set can be very effective.

Setting the stage for *Alice's Adventures*

In a play with many scenes, such as *Alice*, it would be expensive and complicated to show new settings with each scene change. Instead, you should keep things simple by having a plain **backdrop**.

You could just use props and lights to show when the place changes. For example, you could use a green backdrop for all outdoor scenes. For the tea party scene, you can put out a painted cardboard house. This can be taken away when Alice moves on to the croquet scene.

Staging the action gets complicated when Alice grows, shrinks, or moves between places in the same scene. You may not have time to change the scenery! In these cases, it may be easier for the actors to express changes taking place in words.

Costumes

As soon as your play is cast, you need to think about the costumes. If your play is based on a book with pictures, look at those for inspiration. Otherwise look on the Internet to see what clothes the characters in your play could wear.

You should put one or two people in charge of finding and organizing the costumes. As much as possible, borrow clothes or buy them cheaply from thrift stores. You might know someone with sewing skills who can help to make some of the costumes.

Think about how you can use costumes to make the play funny. Look for unusual clothes that stand out and include hats and silly shoes. Some characters might need uniforms or special clothes to reflect the jobs they have.

TRY IT

It might be difficult to find costumes for some characters, such as animal characters. To get around this, and to add humor, actors could wear masks or use makeup to show how the character looks. Animal onesies or hand puppets could also work well!

If one of your characters has a specific job, you might want the costume to show this.

Consider using makeup, as well as costumes, to change the look of your actors.

Costumes for *Alice's Adventures*

Here are some costume suggestions for a few of the characters in *Alice's Adventures*:

* A simple dress for Alice

* A crown and a dress with big red hearts for the Queen of Hearts

* White rabbit ears or makeup and a vest or jacket over plain clothes for White Rabbit

* A sleeping bag for the Caterpillar

* Large hare ears, bow tie, and brown clothes for the March Hare

* A large top hat and bow tie for the Hatter

31

In this play, *Toad of Toad Hall*, the props manager has found a funny way to show Toad driving his car.

Props

Props are the things that actors pick up and move around within the play. For example, when characters eat a meal they need plates, knives, forks, and drinking glasses.

As a director, you need to make sure your actors are using the props in a natural way. Using props should not stop actors from speaking their lines clearly. Also, there should not be too many props onstage—you don't want the stage to look messy.

Use someone as the props manager to be in charge of organizing all the props. This person has a list of the props used in the play and knows which ones are used when. He or she also needs to tell the **stagehands** where things go. Props needs to be set out correctly, so that everything is in the right place for the actors to pick up.

To prepare for your play, start by making a list of all the props you need. Do this as early as you can, because it might take time to find everything. Borrow as many things as possible and keep a list of whom each item belongs to. You might get some other cheap items in a thrift store, or you could make some objects yourselves.

TRY IT

Some plays use no props! The actors mime instead of using objects. You could use mime in this way to make your play funnier. In other plays, actors use the same object for different purposes. For example, a banana could be a pen, a phone, or a sword!

Props for *Alice's Adventures*

Here are some prop ideas you may need for your version of *Alice*:

* Plastic toy food for cakes and cookies

* A child's toy tea-set for the tea party

* Wrap a soft toy pig in a blanket to create the baby that turns into a pig

You don't have to use props at all. You could just mime, or pretend, that there are props. This can be very funny.

Light and sound

If you perform your play in a place with theater-style lights, you'll need someone in charge of lighting. This person is called the lighting manager. He or she can change the color or brightness of the lights onstage or put a spotlight on particular actors. If you don't have any real stage lights, then you just need someone to turn the lights on and off as necessary during the performances.

Lighting effects can really add to the atmosphere onstage.

A slide whistle makes a very funny noise.

You will probably want music and sound effects in your play. Think about how you could use music just before the play starts to let the audience know it is a comedy. However, keep in mind that a lot of popular music is under copyright. This means you have to pay the person who created the music to use it in a performance.

Light and sound effects in *Alice's Adventures*

As the director, you should go through the script with the people in charge of lighting and sound, to discuss what effects should be in each scene. Here are some ideas for the scenes in *Alice*:

Scene 1: Alice falling down the rabbit hole

* Lighting: Start off with a bright light, then slowly dim it
* Sound: Use a **slide whistle** as Alice falls and a cymbal when she lands at the bottom

Scene 2: Alice shrinking, growing, and crying

* Lighting: Spotlight on Alice reduces in brightness as she shrinks and increases in brightness as she grows
* Sound: Use a recording of waves crashing at sea when Alice cries and makes a flood

Scene 3: Alice in different locations

* Lighting: Change colors to show that Alice is in a new place
* Sound: Use fast, crazy music during the Caucus Race

NEARLY READY

You've worked so hard rehearsing your play, and now you're nearly ready to perform it! There are just a few more things to do.

Ways to promote your play

First, remember to **promote** your play so that people know about it and want to see it. If you are performing your play at school, you could ask to put an **advertisement** or an article in your school newsletter or on the school web site. It's a good idea to include some photographs of rehearsals or of the actors in their costumes. This will give people an idea of what the play will be like.

You could also design and give out **fliers**. Hand these out to people a few weeks before the performance. Sell tickets in advance—this will help you get a sense of the number of people attending.

Post information about your play on bulletin boards where people find information on events.

If you can talk about your play on the radio, you can reach lots of possible audience members.

There are other way to spread the word further. Try getting an article or review published in a local newspaper or events web site.

You could also try getting a mention on local radio. You could even have your actors read a particularly funny part of a scene from the play live on air. Make sure you let everyone know how hard you have worked on the play, and that you did it all yourselves.

TRY IT

You could make a video of some highlights from the play and put it on a video-sharing web site. Make sure you have permission from everyone on your team before you do this. Ask an adult to upload the clip for you. You could also ask your teacher or an adult family member to mention the play on **social media**.

MAKING POSTERS

One of the best ways to let many people know about your play is to put posters up everywhere you can! Here's how to do it:

1. Look at other posters for comedies. What have the posters' designers done to show people that the play is funny? Have they just included a funny image, or have they also used a funny **font**? What sorts of words have they used to describe the play?

2. Choose an image for your poster. This could be a photo of the actors performing a funny scene from the play. Perhaps you could draw or paint your own image summing up the message of the play.

3. Think about the text you're going to include on your poster. The title of the play needs to be in large, clear letters that people can see from far away. Choose a bold color for these letters so they stand out.

4. You might want to include a **slogan**. Choose a memorable, short phrase about the play, which will help persuade them to come and see it. For example: "Follow the rabbit into the chaos of Wonderland!"

It is quick and simple to design a poster on a computer.

Alice's Adventures in Wonderland

Directed by Brenda Evans

STARRING

Helen Smith
as Alice

John Price
as The Rabbit

Steve Parker
as The Hatter

In this
style
10/6

Wednesday, March 17—Saturday, March 20, at 8 p.m.
and Saturday, March 20, at 2 p.m.
At Gosford Hill School, Assembly Room
E-mail the main office for your free ticket

title of play

director

people playing the
main characters

where and when
the performance is

how you get tickets

5. Many posters include a comment from people who have seen the play. You could ask a friend or teacher to watch the play in rehearsal. If they like it, include a positive review from them in large letters on the poster. Again, this will help to persuade people that your play is worth seeing.

6. Don't forget to include the dates, times, and place of the performances and the ticket prices (or say it's free).

7. Make color copies of your poster, then post them around your school and neighborhood. Make sure you only put posters up where you have permission!

Getting ready to perform

As the date of your first performance gets nearer, everyone involved in the play will probably start to feel some pressure. You may also be feeling tired after all those rehearsals! There may still be a lot to get ready, but it will be worth it in the end.

It's opening night and people are picking up their tickets. Will you be ready?

First of all, as the director, you should make sure that all the actors have learned their lines properly. It's a good idea to have a **prompt** sitting nearby with a copy of the script during performances, as a safety net. Your play will run much more smoothly and your audience will be impressed if everyone knows his or her lines. Encourage your actors to practice their lines together outside of rehearsals, too.

You'll be rehearsing the play from start to finish by now, but it might still be useful to practice key scenes. This is especially important for more complicated moments that need good comic timing or involve lots of props. All of the actors should feel relaxed and confident with every scene. You do not want them to dread a tricky part they feel they haven't practiced enough.

Now is a good time to make **programs** for the play. These should include information such as the names of the playwright, director, cast members, and the characters they play. There should also be information about the backstage **crew**. The audience may not get to see those people working backstage during the performance, so it's especially important they know about their involvement in the play. This is also a good time to make tickets and arrange the seating for the audience.

THEATER JOB

You'll need to organize some **front-of-house** people to greet the audience at the start of performances. Their job is to take money for tickets, hand out programs, and show people to their seats.

SHOWTIME!

You've done all your preparation, the costumes are ready, the props are lined up, and the actors know their lines. So now it's time to perform your play!

You will probably be feeling nervous, but that's natural. Make sure everyone arrives in plenty of time, so that the actors can get into their costumes or put on makeup and the backstage people can check that everything is working properly. It's a good idea to take a few deep breaths before the play begins. This will help you to feel calm and ready to start.

TRY IT

Find someone to take photos of the performance as well as photos of the people working backstage. When the play has finished, you'll all be glad to have pictures. They will remind you of the play and the wonderful time you had together.

Try to relax and enjoy yourself onstage.

Make sure your actors have time before the play to remember what they practiced in the rehearsals. Remind them to face the audience as they deliver their lines and to speak loudly and clearly. Since you won't be used to having a real audience laughing during your performance, tell your actors to remember to wait for the noise to die down before they say the next line. Don't worry if people make a mistake. The chances are the audience won't even notice. You must not let one mistake get you off track for the rest of the play.

Most importantly, enjoy yourself! Taking part in staging a play is hard work, but it's a lot of fun. It's wonderful to show what you can do as part of a team. Make sure you all take a big bow at the end when the audience is clapping. It will feel amazing!

Don't rush offstage at the end, and make the most of the audience's applause.

GLOSSARY

acrobatics gymnastic skills

advertisement notice or announcement to tell people about a thing or event

audition test for actors to try out for particular roles

backdrop background to a set

cast give actors roles in a play; the collective name for all the actors in a play

catchphrase well-known phrase

Caucus Race race featured in *Alice's Adventures in Wonderland*. All participants have to run in circles until the end is called and everyone is named a winner.

comedy type of entertainment that makes people laugh

comic timing pace of a scene designed to make the audience laugh

crew people working backstage on a play

cue signal to an actor to move or speak

dialogue words actors speak

director person in charge of staging a play

flier small leaflet giving information

font set of letters and symbols in a particular design

front-of-house area of the theater business concerning the audience, such as ticket sales

improvisation sketch made up by actors as they go along

intermission break in the middle of a play

line sentence of dialogue in the script

narrator person who describes and explains what is happening

part role in a play

playwright person who writes the text of the play

plot story of a book, movie, or play

program booklet for audience members giving information about the play, cast, and crew

promote encourage people to like or do something

prompt person whose job is to remind actors of lines they have forgotten

prop object that actors can move around onstage

pun type of joke where the humor occurs because a word has more than one meaning

punchline last line of a joke that is intended to make people laugh

role character or part in a play

script text of the play

set scenery and furniture on the stage

sidekick assistant or close friend

sketch short, funny performance

slapstick type of comedy in which actors behave in a silly way, such as falling over or dropping things

slide whistle musical instrument that makes a funny, sliding sound

slogan memorable phrase to help people remember something

social media web sites where people can share ideas and information

stage direction instruction for an actor in a script

stagehand person who moves scenery and props around during a performance

wordplay activity of joking about the meaning of words in a clever way

FIND OUT MORE

Web sites

FactHound offers a safe, fun way to find Internet sites related to this book. All of the sites on FactHound have been researched by our staff.

Here's all you do:

Visit www.facthound.com
Type in this code: 9781484627693

Most cities and many towns have theater companies that put on plays for kids. Do research to find the theaters near you that offer plays for kids or theater training for young people. Perhaps you could ask if you could visit and look around, or ask about plays that are coming up. Check to see if there are any workshops with the actors or the writers.

Plays to read

Farmer, David. *101 Drama Games and Activities*. Seattle: CreateSpace, 2009.

Young, Rebecca. *Drama Projects for the Middle School Classroom*. Colorado Springs: Meriweather, 2013.

Young, Rebecca. *Ten-Minute Plays for Middle School Performers*. Colorado Springs: Meriweather, 2008.

Think about some classic funny stories, such as the *Frog and Toad* books, *Shrek*, Roald Dahl's stories, or the work of Dr. Seuss. With an adult's help, you can find different stage adaptations of these stories. If you visit your local library, you can also find new funny plays you haven't heard of before.

Drama game

If you enjoyed the "Stop and Talk" improvisation game earlier in the book, perhaps try the following improvisation game, too.

"The 15-Second Game"

Everyone should prepare to act as their character in the play. Once a bell sounds, everyone in the room has 15 seconds to do one of the following things "in character":

- Shake as many hands as possible.

- Surprise someone by tapping him or her on the shoulder.

- Touch the floor and at least two walls with their hands

- Throw a pretend cream pie in people's faces and then apologize.

When time is up, the bell will ring again. Everybody should then form a circle and share their experiences.

INDEX